ABC
of PLACES and THINGS in the BIBLE
Child's Workbook
(Ages 9-10)

BY

© Oluwakemi O.Ola-Ojo 2011

ABC of Places and Things in the Bible - Child's Workbook 1.

ISBN – 978-1-908015-03-7
© 2011 by Oluwakemi O. Ola-Ojo

All publishing rights belong exclusively to Protokos Publishers.

Published by:
Protokos Publishers
PO Box 48424
London
SE15 2YL
United Kingdom
Website: www.protokospublishers.co.uk
E-Mail: admin@protokospublishers.co.uk

Printed in the United Kingdom. All rights reserved under International Copyright Law. Contents and/or cover may not be reproduced in whole or in part in any form without the express written consent of the Publisher.

Introduction:

This is the 2nd of a 2-part series. Book one is for the parent/teacher and book two is for the child. We recommend teaching only an alphabet per week and conscious efforts should be made by the parent/teacher to do the exercise with the child all through the week. We need to train/teach the child line-by-line, precept upon precept. Every alphabet has been written up with some ideas. We would recommend that the parent/teacher uses only what is applicable for the child and pitch the teaching to the child's level of understanding.

In book two the same story is written in simple English for the child to read to the parent/teacher, the aim of which is to help him/her learn to read. The child can write, draw and colour what he/she has drawn. The reading could be done daily as the child's bedtime story. It is meant to reinforce what has been taught previously. Effectively this is the child's workbook.

Allow the child a break if he or she is tired while working on the workbook. Praise child for his or her effort, however little.

The parent/teacher should assess the child's performance in the reading, writing and drawing by ticking the most appropriate commendation at the end of the 'time to draw page'.

This workbook belongs to:

----

of address:

Date:_____ / _____ /20_____

Time to practice how to write.

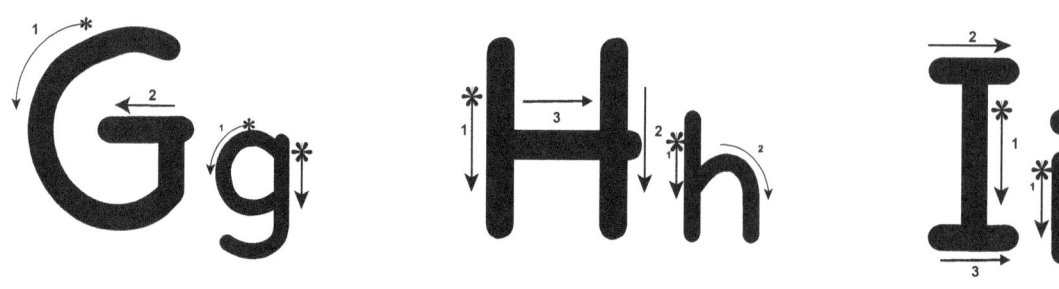

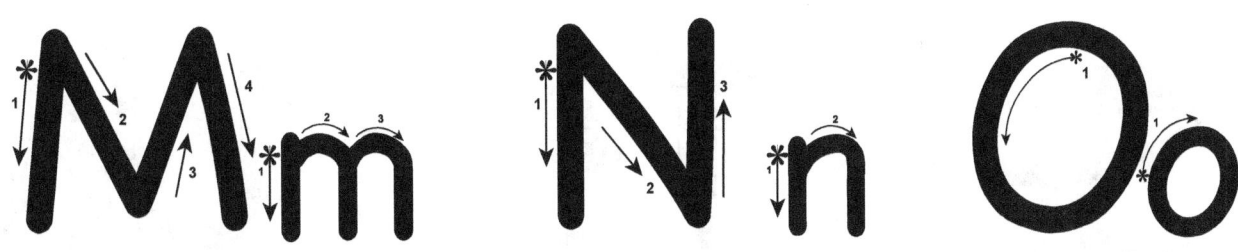

 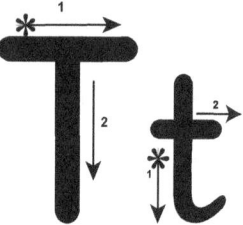 

8

Time to read:

A is for the ark.
God told Noah to build an ark.
The ark was for him and his family.
The ark was to provide room for animals and birds, in pairs.
Noah obeyed God in everything and the floods came.
All that was in the ark with Noah were saved.

Time to write:

A is for the ark.

A is for the Ark.

God told Noah to build an ark.

Noah obeyed God and the floods came.

Time to draw:

Draw Noah in the ark together with the animals in the ark.

Well done ☐
Good Job ☐
Excellent ☐

Time to read:

B is for the basket.
Boys were to be killed when Moses was born.
His parents hid him so that he would not die.
His mother made him a beautiful basket.
She placed Moses in the basket among the reeds.
The princess found Moses and spared his life.

Time to write:

B is for the basket.

B is for the Basket.

Boys were to be killed when Moses was born.

The princess found Moses and spared his life.

Time to draw:

Draw baby Moses in a basket on the river.

Well done ☐
Good Job ☐
Excellent ☐

Time to read:

C is for camels.
Abraham's trusted servant went on a trip to Ur.
He travelled a long distance to Ur with ten camels.
He made the camels kneel by the well outside the city and prayed.
Rebecca gave him water to drink and offered water to the camels.
Rebecca actually ran and gave water to the ten camels.

Time to write:

C is for Camels.

C is for Camels.

Abraham's trusted servant went on a trip to Ur.

Rebecca ran and gave water to the ten camels.

Time to draw:

Draw Rebecca trying to give water to the camels.

Well done ☐
Good Job ☐
Excellent ☐

Time to read:

D is for the donkey.
This donkey belonged to a man called Balaam.
Balaam beat this donkey one day as they went out.
This donkey asked its master why it was beaten.
Unlike many other donkeys this monkey saw an angel.
This donkey protected the life of its master Balaam.

Time to write:

D is for the Donkey.

D is for the Donkey.

This donkey belonged to a man called Balaam.

This donkey protected the life of Balaam.

Time to draw:

Draw the donkey talking with Balaam.

Well done ☐
Good Job ☐
Excellent ☐

Time to read:

E is for Emmaus.
Emmaus was about seven miles away from Jerusalem.
One day two men walked from Jerusalem to Emmaus.
On their way a stranger joined them and spoke with them.
The stranger clearly explained the Bible to the two men.
The men did not know that it was Jesus Christ speaking

Time to write:

E is for Emmaus.

E is for Emmaus.

Two men walked from Jerusalem to Emmaus.

On their way a stranger spoke with them.

Time to draw:

Draw Jesus Christ speaking to the two men.

Well done ☐
Good Job ☐
Excellent ☐

Time to read:

F is for the fish Peter caught.
Jesus Christ had no money to pay his tax.
Jesus Christ told Peter to go to the sea and fish.
There was to be enough money in the mouth of the first fish.
Peter obeyed Jesus and went with his hook a-fishing.
Peter caught the first fish and in its mouth was enough money.

Time to write:

F is for the fish Peter caught.

F is for the **F**ish Peter caught.

Jesus told Peter to go to the sea and fish.

Peter found money in the mouth of the fish.

Time to draw:

Draw Peter taking money out of the mouth of the fish.

Well done ☐
Good Job ☐
Excellent ☐

Time to read:

G is for Galilee.
Jesus Christ died and after three days He rose from the dead.
His disciples went to meet Him in Galilee after this.
Jesus Christ spoke with them and prayed for them.
At Galilee the disciples saw Jesus Christ going up in the sky.
The angels told them Jesus Christ would someday come back.

Time to write:

G is for Galilee.

G is for Galilee.

At Galilee Jesus Christ went up in the sky.

Jesus Christ would someday come back.

Time to draw:

Draw the angels talking to the disciples.

Well done ☐
Good Job ☐
Excellent ☐

Time to read:

H is for heaven.
God made the heaven and the earth.
God and His angels live in heaven.
Heaven is a very beautiful place with streets of gold.
In heaven there is no hunger, thirst, sorrow or sickness.
Those who believe in Jesus go to heaven when they die.

Time to write:

H is for Heaven.

H is for **H**eaven.

God made the heaven and the earth.

God and His angels live in heaven.

Time to draw:

Draw heaven and the streets of gold.

Well done ☐
Good Job ☐
Excellent ☐

Time to read:

I is for the Island of Patmos.
An island is a dry land surrounded by water.
John lived on the island of Patmos for some time.
In Patmos, an angel of God appeared and spoke to John.
John wrote to the people in the seven churches.
John wrote all that he saw in the last book of the Bible.

Time to write:

I is for the Island of Patmos.

I is for the Island of Patmos.

An island is a dry land surrounded by water.

John lived on the island of Patmos for some time.

Time to draw:

Draw John writing on the Island.

Well done ☐
Good Job ☐
Excellent ☐

Time to read:

J is for Joppa.
Dorcas lived in Joppa.
Joppa was a seaside town.
Jonah took a ship from Joppa.
Many ships took off from Joppa.
Peter's friend also lived in Joppa.

Time to write:

J is for Joppa.

J is for Joppa.

Joppa was a seaside town.

Many ships took off from Joppa.

Time to draw:

Draw a seaside town called Joppa.

Well done ☐
Good Job ☐
Excellent ☐

Time to read:

K is for Kidron.
Kidron was a brook.
Kidron brook was used for burning idols.
Kidron brook was just outside of Jerusalem.
King Asa burnt all his mother's idols at the Kidron brook.
King Solomon told Shimei not to cross the Kidron brook.

Time to write:

K is for Kidron.

K is for Kidron.

Kidron was a brook.

Kidron brook was just outside of Jerusalem.

Time to draw:
Draw a brook.

Well done ☐
Good Job ☐
Excellent ☐

Time to read:

L is for lion's den.
A den is a caged area for the lions.
Lions were kept in the den in the time of Daniel.
Daniel was thrown into the lion's den but he came out uninjured.
It is dangerous for any child to play with a lion.
We can see the lion's den today in the animal zoo.

Time to write:

L is for Lion's den.

L is for Lion's den.

We can see the lion today in the animal zoo.

It is dangerous for any child to play with a lion.

Time to draw:
Draw a lion in its den.

Well done ☐
Good Job ☐
Excellent ☐

Time to read:

M is for Macedonia.
Paul had a vision to go to Macedonia.
Paul took Timothy with him to Macedonia.
Paul set up many Churches in Macedonia and beyond.
Christians in Macedonia gave some money to the poor.
Paul preached about Jesus Christ to many people in Macedonia.

Time to write:

M is for Macedonia.

M is for Macedonia.

Paul had a vision to go to Macedonia.

Paul took Timothy with him to Macedonia.

Time to draw:

Draw Paul and Timothy preaching in Macedonia.

Well done ☐
Good Job ☐
Excellent ☐

Time to read:

N is for Nineveh.
Nineveh was a great city.
The people of Nineveh sinned against the Lord.
God told Jonah to go and preach to the people in Nineveh,
Jonah ran away to Tarshish but was swallowed by a big fish.
God made the fish to vomit Jonah near Nineveh City.

Time to write:

N is for Nineveh.

N is for Nineveh.

Nineveh was a great city.

The people of Nineveh sinned against the Lord.

Time to draw:

Draw Jonah praying inside the belly of the big fish.

Well done ☐
Good Job ☐
Excellent ☐

Time to read:

O is for olive leaf.
The olive leaf is from the olive tree.
Olive trees live for hundreds of years.
The second dove brought an olive leaf to Noah in the ark.
The olive leaf confirmed to Noah that there was life again.
King Solomon used olive tree in building the temple.

Time to write:

O is for Olive leaf.

O is for Olive leaf.

The olive leaf is from the olive tree.

Olive trees live for hundreds of years.

Time to draw:

Draw the dove giving an olive leaf to Noah in the ark.

Well done ☐
Good Job ☐
Excellent ☐

Time to read:

P is for Passover.
God ordained the Passover feast.
Passover feast was to be remembered yearly.
Passover lamb was to be roasted and eaten in a hurry.
Passover was the time the Lord protected the Israelites.
Passover feast was to be mentioned to the future generations.

Time to write:

P is for Passover.

P is for Passover.

God ordained the Passover feast.

Passover feast was to be remembered yearly.

Time to draw:

Draw people feasting or having a barbeque.

Well done ☐
Good Job ☐
Excellent ☐

Time to read:

Q is for quails.
Quails are small, low flying birds.
Quails are very delicious and nutritional birds.
God sent many quails to the Israelites camp, daily.
Quails were very easy to catch in the time of Moses.
The Israelites ate quails for forty years in the evenings.

Time to write:

Q is for Quails.

Q is for Quails.

Quails are small, low flying birds.

Quails are very delicious and nutritional birds.

Time to draw:

Draw the people catching quails.

Well done ☐
Good Job ☐
Excellent ☐

Time to read:

R is for rainbow.
God placed the rainbow in the sky.
The rainbow has many lovely colours.
The rainbow is always like a half circle.
The rainbow is a covenant sign from God to us.
The rainbow reminds us of God's love to mankind.

Time to write:

R is for Rainbow.

R is for Rainbow.

God placed the rainbow in the sky.

The rainbow has many lovely colours.

Time to draw:

Draw a rainbow.

Well done ☐
Good Job ☐
Excellent ☐

Time to read:

S is for the sun.
The sun gives light to us all.
The sun divides the day from the night.
God created the Sun on the fourth day.
The sun helps us to know days, months and seasons.
The sun keeps us warm especially when we are outside.

Time to write:

S is for the Sun.

S is for the Sun.

God created the Sun on the fourth day.

The sun divides the day from the night.

Time to draw:

Draw the Sun shining on people.

Well done ☐
Good Job ☐
Excellent ☐

Time to read:

T is for the Ten Commandments.
The Ten Commandments are from God.
The Ten Commandments help us to live safely.
The Ten Commandments are to help us live right.
The Ten Commandments teach us to obey our parents.
The Ten Commandments help us to know how to relate to God.

Time to write:

T is for the Ten Commandments.

T is for the Ten Commandments.

The Ten Commandments are from God.

The Commandments are to help us live right.

Time to draw:

Draw Moses holding the Ten Commandments.

Well done ☐
Good Job ☐
Excellent ☐

Time to read:

U is for Ur.
The Chaldees lived in the land of Ur.
Abram's family were originally from Ur.
Abram's parents, brothers and sisters all lived in Ur.
They were a happy family living in Ur.
One day God spoke to Abram to leave Ur.

Time to write:

U is for Ur.

U is for Ur.

The Chaldees lived in the land of Ur.

Abram's family were originally from Ur.

Time to draw:

Draw Abram's family in Ur.

Well done □
Good Job □
Excellent □

Time to read:

V is for Valley.
A valley is the deep/hollow between two hills.
One day God, in a vision, showed Ezekiel a valley.
The valley was full of very dry bones.
God asked Ezekiel to speak to the dry bones.
God made people out of the dry bones in the valley.

Time to write:

V is for Valley.

V is for Valley.

A valley is the deep/hollow between two hills.

God made people out of the dry bones.

Time to draw:

Draw Ezekiel speaking to dry bones in the valley.

Well done ☐
Good Job ☐
Excellent ☐

Time to read:

W is for water.
We drink water and cook with water.
We wash ourselves, our clothes, our cars with water.
There were six empty water pots at the wedding.
Jesus Christ turned water into wine at Cana.
And "it turned out to be a better wine", said the best man.

Time to write:

W is water.

| **W** is for water. |

| |

We drink water and cook with water.

| |

| |

Jesus Christ turned water into wine at Cana.

| |

| |

Time to draw:

Draw a wedding party with six water pots.

Well done ☐
Good Job ☐
Excellent ☐

Time to read:

X is for Exile.
God wants to be their God always.
God gave His commandments to the Israelites.
Disobeying God would lead to captivity.
Exile is where you are forced to be against your will.
Daniel and his friends too were taken into exile.

Time to write:

X is for exile.

X is for Exile.

God wants to be their God always.

Disobeying God will lead to captivity.

Time to draw:

Draw Daniel and his friends taken into captivity.

Well done ☐
Good Job ☐
Excellent ☐

Time to read:

Y is for yeast.
Yeast has small grains.
Yeast is sold in the food shops.
Yeast makes the dough to get bigger.
Yeast is one of the things used for making bread.
Yeast works quietly on the flour that is used in making bread.

Time to write:

Y is for Yeast.

Y is for Yeast.

Yeast has small grains.

Yeast is sold in the food shops.

Time to draw:

Draw grains of yeast in a bowl next to a bag of flour.

Well done ☐
Good Job ☐
Excellent ☐

Time to read:

Z is for mount Zion.
Mount Zion is located within Jerusalem.
Mount Zion is also called the city of David.
David lived in the fortified city of Mount Zion.
Many security men guarded King David in Mount Zion.
The ark was kept in mount Zion during the time of King David.

Time to write:

Z is for mount Zion.

| Z is for mount Zion. |

| |

Mount Zion is located within Jerusalem.

| |

| |

Mount Zion is also called the city of David.

| |

| |

Time to draw:

Draw Mount Zion at the time of King David.

Well done ☐
Good Job ☐
Excellent ☐

How to become God's child and friend:

Please say this prayer:

Dear Lord, thank You for my life. I am sorry for all the bad things that I have said or done. Please forgive me for all these bad things.

Lord, I want to be Your child and friend from now on. Please come into my heart and forgive me for all the bad things that I have said and done. From now, please be my Lord and Friend and teach me Your ways in Jesus name I pray. Amen

Coming out Soon

- **A.B.C. OF PEOPLE AND THINGS IN THE BIBLE BOOK 2 SERIES**
- **A.B.C. OF PLACES AND THINGS IN THE BIBLE BOOK 2 SERIES**